I DEAL IDEAS

ADMINISTRATIVE IDEAS

PONNADA NAGA SURENDRA

Copyright © Ponnada Naga Surendra
All Rights Reserved.

THANKS to the beloved

RAYUDU, BHAVANI, RAMYA and SRI GARU.

DEDICATED TO

"SiTaRa"

Contents

Preface

"The main purpose of publishing this book is not for seeking any praise from somebody or to become popular. There are many readers in our country and states who like to read those books written by their favourite authors. My solely hope is that I want authors to write a book and publish it in the name of an old age home or orphanage account. Need to see, when the book is taken by someone then the money should be deposited directly in orphanage's bank account. If your book sells more than the expected then there is no need for that orphanage or nursing home to wait for funds. Taking this as an initiative, I am publishing this book in the name of an organisation. A good book can increase a person's life moments. Thanks to RAYUDU, SRI, BHAVANI AND RAMYA."

With regards,

Acknowledgements

"I have to start by thanking my friends, colleagues and my parents. From going through early drafts and giving me the advices on the cover. so I could edit and present it before you. Thank you so much. I would not be in this position if you did not inflence and motivate me."

Prologue

INTRODUCTION:-

"This book deals with unimaginable situations that are being faced by many states all over India. Here, this book provides solutions to some of the problems that are present in our society. Some of the problems can't be executed due to lack of budgetary problems. Some of the problems are already in execution but I have advanced those solutions. Some of the points in this book is not clearly explained as most of the details are not quite clear, understanding and getting information regarding a topic is not sooth."

Main theme of this book is no blaming or criticizing any government. The only thing is, "if a person with determination and skill wants to serve his country then how he could strive hard so as to find solutions to problems in this society." This is completely a frictional book. The contents of this book can also be used in real life for the well-being of society. Some things have been Extracted from Google.

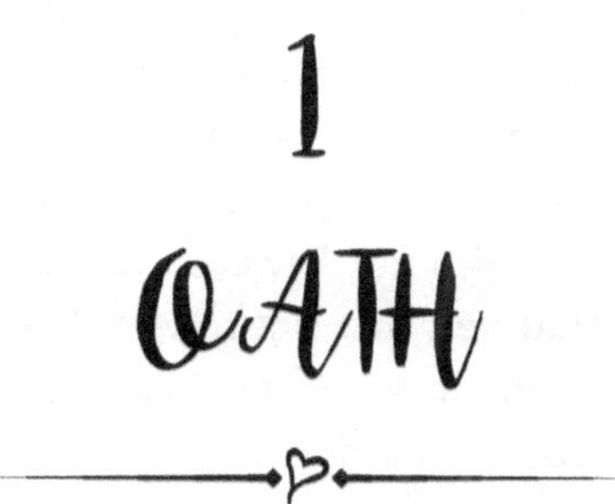

1

OATH

(Ceremony)

Word Introduction: -

"Many hardships, many insults and many revolutionary decisions all together put me before you as Chief Minister this time. When my conscience asked me to do something for the sake of my country, I changed my way of thinking and behaviour and came into politics. Everyone, with whom I spent had taught me great lessons and responsibilities. They might not be responsible for my life, but they were responsible for my responsibility."

Content Analysis: -

(In mind)

"People were waiting with anticipation that I was going to do something as Chief Minister for the sake of their livelihood and overall development. I should not act as a Fence or barrier for their aspirations and dreams. Many glances were on my side with optimism. Since they had gone through pessimistic conditions in their past, they believed that our government would not drag their standard of their subsistence. As a result, I believed that they not only cast their votes for me but also their belief and faith on me. Meanwhile, I was called for my swearing-in as Chief Minister."

Constitutional standard: -

"Constructed by the 'I ..... I' inscription towards the Constitution of India. I will show true faith and allegiance, I will carry out my duties as the Chief Minister of the State with care and conscientiousness to safeguard the sovereignty and integrity of India, without fear, without partiality, without any hatred I swear by God that I will bring justice to all people under the

Constitution and the law."

Whistles and carnations around !!!

My heartfelt greetings to the guests who attended the swearing-in ceremony, to my well-wishers who came, to the Governor and the Chief Ministers of other states. I was forever indebted to all the people who believed in me and walked with me. I swear this government would provide successful governance that you had never seen before. Everyone was very much looking forward at me in an enthusiasm on what my first signature would be on as mentioned in a manifesto.

The first signature I'm progressing to place on is making all sanitation workers permanent. We will hold a separate press conference tomorrow at 3 p.m. and will explain about this matter in detail.

I hope that you will work with me as an individual and as a group for the prosperity of our state and travel with me to uphold this state at the highest level in the country.

Now I'm taking a holiday.

I could not sleep that night because of one reason, 'I was filled with overwhelming while remembering the meeting that took place today and the second was, I felt like that I should make very good decisions and strive for their well-being.'

"The chuckle sound in the morning made me realise that my conscience was reborn to reinvent and renovate new life and new things in this society for my beloved people."

"For yesterday's competition,
For today's power,
For tomorrow's domination,
There is only solution,
That is our culture. "

It's about 3 in the afternoon ....

I started saying so My heartfelt greetings to the trade union leaders, municipal presidents, journalists and cabinet ministers who came to this press meet. otherday, Like I said I make sanitation workers all permanent.

Incentives: -

- I am increasing their next month's salary from 15 thousand to 25 thousand. HRA, EPF all go together 20 thousand will be in their hands.
- We will provide free meals to them at government-established dining centres.

- Their health check-ups are done every two weeks.
- We are going to give free education to their children and scholarships to study in other countries. Free education means that they can continue their education at any school (private but government) and college where they want to study.
- Insurance covers Rs 5 lakh per worker. Only for those who died in the service.
- We provide higher education to their children without any hindrance in recognition of the services rendered by them even after the death of a person.
- We give salaries appropriate to their difficulty, regardless of caste.

Responsibilities you have to perform: -

We are going to give you some more responsibilities regardless of what you are currently doing

- Responsibility of daily watering and taking care of trees. Planting trees and protecting city and nascent areas from pollution and global warming. Every public and private land in the state should be kept green.
- Some even have to act like spies if asked elsewhere.
- Dynamic structures where you work, even if there is a problem with the drainage or the road is damaged, the problem should be brought to the attention of the authorities immediately and a solution should be found. We need to see people not to run to our office for the solution to their troubles.
- If necessary, you need to paint the roads during the summer when the sun is burning, without disturbing the passengers, take care of everything by setting up Water pots.
- Take care not to stagnate water anywhere during the rainy season.
- Sometimes, night workers have to work as guards.
- They have to clean the roads as well as the tourist area places.
- Whoever, interested in painting and art design, have to draw pictures and sayings of great personality on the walls on either side of the road. The benefit of this is that people from all around the world comes to us for scenic beauty.
- Everyone should work for12 hours a day.
- Bonuses and salaries will be given depending on the work they do.

Health Benefits: -

- For women, two days leave during menstruation and for pregnant women, six months paid leave. Total holidays are supposed to be five days per month for women and three days for men.
- Those who have been in this profession for 7 years will be given Regular-Permanent in the cadre. For them, free medical care for their children, health check-ups will be provided by the government.
- Only those under the age of seven who are perceived to be under Pre-Permanent will be offered free medical care and a health check.

Conclusion: -
"We should Clean up our thoughts, if we think that sanitary workers won't know how to clean."

2
CABINET

Introduction: -

I told everyone there would be a cabinet meeting after the press conference. I know my cabinet ministers would work better than me if they had ideas like mine but, whose mentality was unpredictable.

Need to know something means this meeting was what I needed the most.

Everyone says the future of the state depends on the chief minister, but the future of the state rests on the entire cabinet of ministers. I began to fear how the king would be politicized if the cabinet wanted corruption.

Meanwhile, it was reported that everyone had come to the cabinet meeting.

"My heartfelt greetings to everyone who was sworn in before the Governor as Cabinet Ministers. We have very little contact with you after winning, but today I will talk with you about the will of our government, development welfare. Our winning is not about 3 or 4 places. We won on the idea that people do want us an opponent."

Meanwhile, someone got up

"Rising Sun, youare,

With words like exciting rays,

This state is green with our activists like green leaves," he said.

The only thing I expect from all of you is that you should refrain from praising me.

The good that we can do for the people through your victory should be told to their future generations. Everyone must serve the people with commitment, discipline and perseverance. This is the ultimate goal of everyone. I want to give good governance to the people, first and foremost from our cabinet, then to the MLA, MLC, some suggestions and some things as the Chief Minister. Hence, the first Government Order that I will issue, rather than my first signature.

"For each Cabinet Minister, MLAs and MLCs should select a few and form a team. Those elected should include a Personal assistant, an Experienced doctor in that constituency, an experienced Teacher, a Lawyer, a Business accountant, an Economic expert, a Planning expert, a Farmer on behalf of the Farming community, an Agriculture specialist and the Police."

All of them should have a good understanding and grasp of the issues in their respective branches. This means that the benefit to us, the people, is that people from the different departments can solve that problem very quickly with advice.

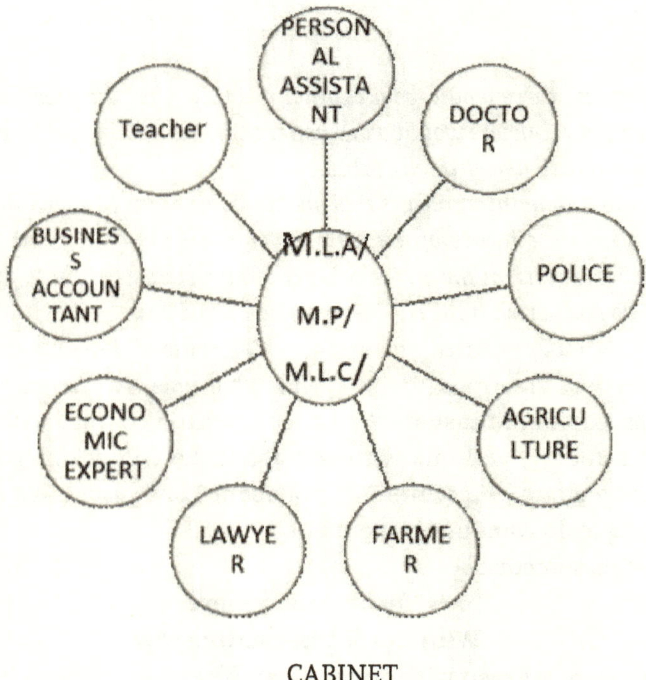

CABINET

• Even if you are elected by the people here, you may not be aware in some branch that you want to do. In our Constitution, MLA's and MP's do not have the power to select such persons. But our government gives them on basis of job laws and always keeps them as help, to the public servant. That is, when a farmer has a problem, these people have to think what kind of problems does a farmer go through and they have to sort out those. An Economic Expert thinks problems related to financial issues.on the other hand, that advice can also be given by police on cases of misconduct against farmers. So, based on this, a problem can be solved that arised from different branches. Similarly, the rest of the department should also advise without any difficulty and see to it that they are implemented. Seen in this way, there are close to twelve hundred advisers for every 100 MLAs and 20 MPs. Through it, the method adopted by the government and the decisions taken can be taken care of by anyone.

The second important point: -

- "Since, we started the government today, we need to tell the people every detail about what the previous government did, how much the previous government spent on welfare and development, the current budget and what it does in the constituency. you need to explain to the people what their government is going to do next, about development, unemployment, the economy, welfare schemes. After that, you need to let people know everything about the activities you are going to do in the next six months. Six months later, you have to tell them all about the program and development work you have done. If development work is not completed as you said you should let them know why you did not do it. We need to listen to their problems and increase their trust in us."
- Everything should go to the people and put it like a meeting and repeat. Journalists should not be called out or press notes should not be issued as well as suggestions from the public and their plight should be listened to with great calmness and an appropriate solution to their plight should be shown.
- Every MLA should reduce the convoy they have and make it easy for the people.
- Remember that the ultimate goal of all of us is to know the full details of what people are up to if they are dissatisfied with anything and to offer them a happy life.
- In the present as in the past, MLAs, MPs, CMs and government employees need to act as a nest to know the performance and to know the hardships of those people. Efforts should be made to reduce corruption to a great extent by acting under the guise of preventing corruption anywhere in the offices.
- Our cabinet meeting would be for 10 times in a month.

Conclusion: -

A system is either the government, but it depends on the decisions we make and the things we do.

"People left us here with a single drop of ink. Remember, if the same ink drop under the scar can lead to personality and person collapse."

We will talk about some current issues in women's security, defence, medicine, education in the next meeting.

That's all for today's cabinet meeting. The next meeting is scheduled for Monday.

Mrs Satya Garu, Ministry of Women and Child Development would like to come forward with an idea of what security measures we can take for the safety and protection of women.

My directives to understand and implement our cabinet seem very vague, but I want my people to be happy and prosperous in this complex society.

Let's wait until Monday. We can analyse and find out what my ministers are thinking and whether they are ready to work continuously for the development of our state.

3

WOMEN SAFETY

(Monday morning)

Good morning, My regards to everyone who came here.

In this meeting, we are going to discuss issues and solutions related to women's safety. I want everyone to talk, so that it will be easier for us to solve those problems and get a better solution at any time.

I request Mrs Satya Gari, to start this session with a documentary and the information obtained for women safety.

Thank you, sir, glad to be working with this party.

Introduction: -

"No matter how much care every state in the country takes, somewhere, somehow women feel insecure. Solving This is a difficult task because protecting a girl everywhere at home and on the streets is not an easy task. It requires special efforts and also support from people."

Most of the people deny putting a CCTV camera on them, as it was completely against Right to Privacy. Sorting out a social problem with limitations is not a sooth way to handle. After spending maximum time, I came here with an idea. Saying so, she gave her perspectives.

"The advice what she gave was good, but there were some mistakes in it. Later discussing those ideas. Everyone in the cabinet was asked for their opinion regarding this idea. we had come to an opinion."

Content Analysis: -

"Drones are being used to protect women during the day. But, giving protection at night means, that it is a little harder and to give protection to those who work in a big industry is one of the hardest things. Despite police patrolling, it is mostly a difficult task in the dark. So, if you think well, a girl has to cross 3 steps to reach home from the office."

- Origin (beginning).
- Vehicle/approach (walking).
- Destination.

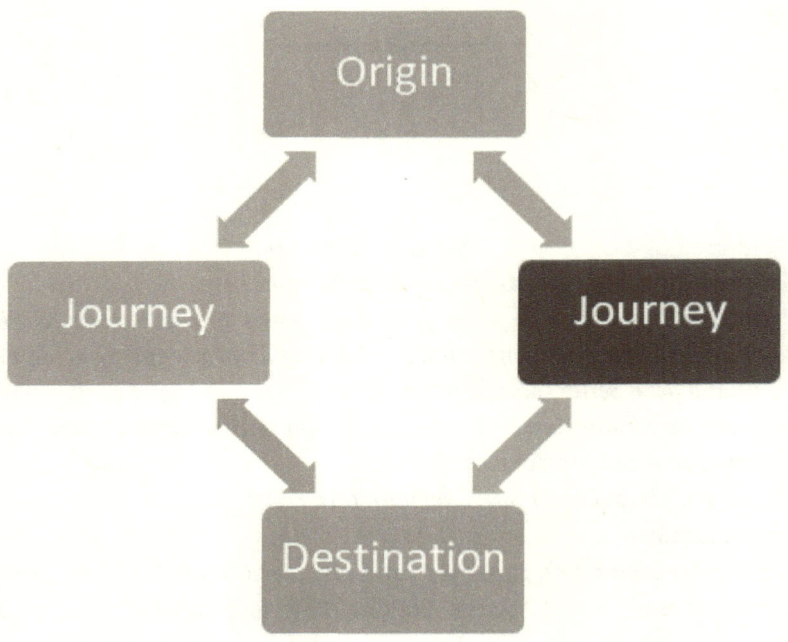

JOURNEY FLOW CHART

There will be no trouble near the start and home. The left-over thing is Moving vehicle.

Vehicles include, "a scooter, on foot and a car."

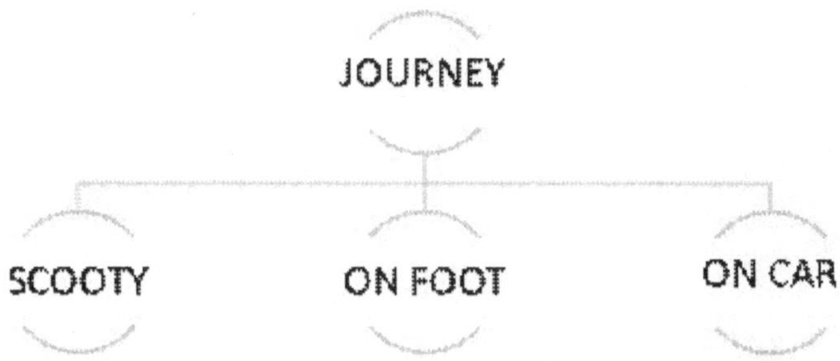

MODE OF JOURNEY

Let's talk about Scooty: -

- Before leaving on Scooty, one must share one's live location with those who are friends, family and supportive.
- Giving a transgender a job like a CC camera. It means, "there are some nodal points on each road, which means there can be a centre connecting 2 roads, a centre connecting 4 roads. Our solution is placing a transgender at that point as a custodian."

For example, let's think of a girl who has an office but has to go from one place to another on scooty. Before leaving that place, she has to register or give her bike number and share her number or mail with that transgender who is present at initial stage in her journey. Then that transgender sends the cart number to the Kinnear on the road that she has mentioned earlier, through which the girl goes home from the office. when she reaches her destination, she has to sign in the registered book saying so that the journey is complete and safe. Through this, we are protecting the profession women with the help of transgenders.

- Night cc cameras and drones should be used where necessary.
- If using a cart, start from 0 km.

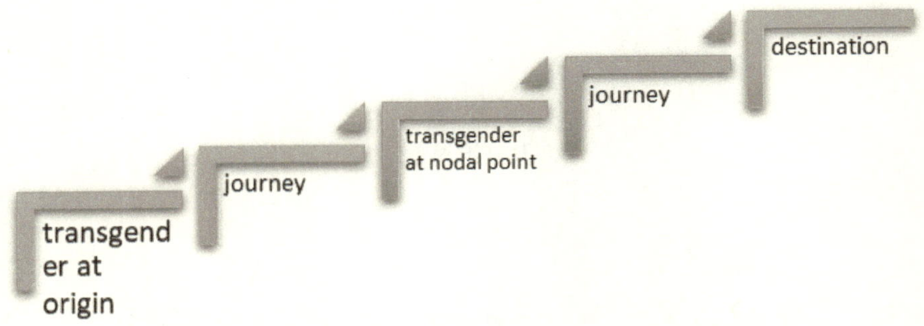

PROCESS FLOWCHART

Second, those who walk: -

- They must also send the location in advance.
- You can go home talking to them on the phone.
- You also have an option to tell transgender, just before the cart says so. Then transgender will give a small machine which she has to take throughout her journey. Females can give that small machine to the transgender that are present nearer to their destination.

Third party booked cab or another vehicle: -

- The first step I will take is, to teach free driving to LGBT related people in the state and take steps to get them jobs in Ola and Uber. The LGBT are providing security for women by giving them jobs in these driving related companies without any hassle.
- Sensor and scan devices are to be installed in every Uber and Ola cabs. This allows anyone booking from the app has to take their details and be allowed in cab only if scanned by Aadhaar card scan or any other identity. just same as, artificial ticket scanner in Metro. They will scan the Aadhaar bar code and inform their details to the cab company and take care from start to finish.
- Caps are also fitted with GPS settings so that they can fully know the details of the cab where it is and where the customer is being taken.
- After booking in the cab, ask for a selfie with the girl in the first stage. It will be useful for the driver. You can end your journey by saying "I am

safe" and "Selfie" at the last stage. All this must be filled set in the booked application. more important thing is this applicated should be monitored at maximum care.

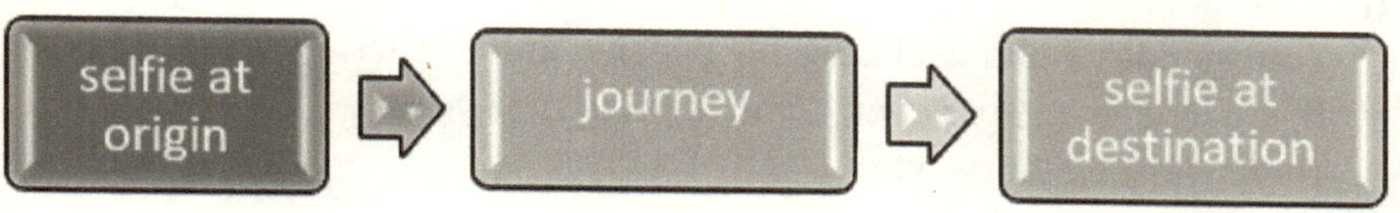

APPLICATION USAGE FLOWCHART

- Sometimes the latter may not be LGBT or less in number, so at such a time, someone as a volunteer can be hired in this process if a woman comes for protection. The same can be done under the internship. certificate to those volunteers are considered as 1st priority during state government jobs.

"Students in every school, from 12 to 18 years, are called adolescents. For them, not only education but also sex education need to be taught. Periods for girls at that age, ethics, the difficulties a girl faces during pregnancy, and the suffering of a women who has been subjected to adultery should all be taught in full. They should be told that everything that happens in society is beaded."

Report: -
Bowls and Hijras in India = 4,87,803 (5,00,000).
Panchayats in all of India = 2,60,000.
Hijras but transgenders in each panchayat = 5,00,000 / 2,60,000 = 2.
transgenders in total 20,000 panchayats = 20,000 x 2 = 40,000.
Those who want to get out of transgender's driving job will be given a night shift of up to 80 per cent and a day shift of up to 20 per cent. This percentage applies to each company.
For now, let's talk about two big companies
Uber first
Drivers working at Uber = 3,00,000.
Those working under the driver in Ola = 5,50,000.

At the moment we only employ transgenders in Uber or Ola companies in some places and if the results are better than expected, we will start everywhere.

An exemption should be given to transgender and children in transgenders.

Transgender = 10% in children between 0 and 6 years

If you look at a 15 per cent, if you look up to 18 years

Total transgender people

= 0.15 X 40,000 = 6,000.

6,000 children are exempt, while the rest = 34,000.

This is one of the solutions for women's safety. But there are some problems with these ideas.

The first thing is, can we guarantee that information about women, will not be transferred to a third party?

Then one of our ministers stood up and asked why we could not issue cards like bus pass cards with special number on it if they really wanted. So, other information would not be transferred to any third party.

These solutions were accepted by all.

Conclusion: -

"The main purpose of our government is to enlist the help of demigods to save women and give them a better life."

After hearing her presentation and our ministers support with their solution I really felt happy for two things.

1. *I could progress welfare of my state with the help of our cabinet ministers.*
2. *Our cabinet was far better than chief minister ideas.*

At the next Cabinet meeting, I would like to ask Mr. Suresh to analyse and represent the current situation and solutions regarding Police on behalf of our police system.

Thanks to everyone. The next cabinet meeting is scheduled for Friday.

(That night)

"The enchanting stars are not the brightest shining stars, but the people who are looking forward to develop our society."

Maintaining the post of Chief Minister was not an easy task, it required a lot of effort and working overnight.

Then I called my personal assistant, and asked him to reschedule my tomorrow's events. He did, as I told.

The next morning, I reached the market yard as a spy and gathered information about what my people really expected from my government and from my side.

They did not really want a luxurious life, I was surprised because they just expected Food, Health, Employment and Education. Even though, they were the minimum basic requirements, why were they looking for them? I mean. So, it was my duty to dig deeper into this issue for the people.

One of the news channels badly reported that the rate of traffic violations had increased in our state. Opposition groups were hoping for a boycott of the Assembly. So, I called the Home Minister to resolve this issue.

4
DEFENCE

(On Friday morning)

My personal assistant called me to a cabinet meeting. I joined them.

They all greeted me with joy. My conscience also believed that something good might happen on that day.

Then the meeting began ...

The home minister stood up and began his presentation.

Word Introduction: -

"We have enormous faith and courage in the police system. Most of the police in our state are doing their duty diligently. Along with the duties they are doing, the new law that we are going to bring in is so far, police system has been into two divisions, and we are dividing them into three divisions."

- Central Government.
- State Government.
- Department of State and Central Government.

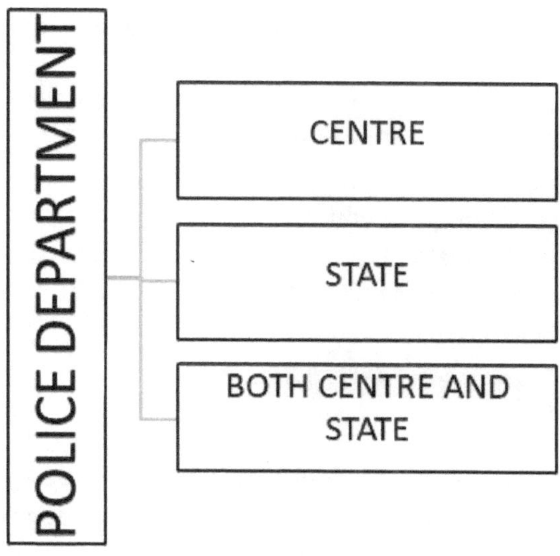

- Employees who are on behalf of the State and Central Government were performing their duties. But the guards of the Centre and the State Department must constantly educate the public. Demos, presentations should be made to aware public and the value of the law to the people, children, friends and women, as well as the Indian panel codes contained in it. The issues related to how to move forward in the difficulties and in plight. We will appoint a Centrally Appointed IPS Officer, as the Head of this State and Central Government Department. Get close to every single thing he does, be successful, advise if necessary and take reports from time to time.

- Like medical camps, police camps should be held 2-3 times a week in each panchayat.

- Measures will be taken to provide free education and free employment opportunities to their children who are serving in the Army or Navy. We will see to it that their children travel by bus for free, no matter where they are in the state.

- As the train falls under the purview of the Central Government, the students or their family members using the train should inform the State Government in advance of the reason for their departure. The state government will take the ticket depending on their needs. This way, it is a free facility for the family members of the soldiers. This only applies 4 times a month.

- Domestic products can be taken for free up to Rs 6 lakh per month.
- If any soldier is found guilty of wrongdoing in the Navy, they will seize the property and recover whatever interest is expended on them by the Government excluding the education of one child.
- In the event of the death of the same hero, we will provide free education, medical care and free bus service to any family in the state for the rest of their lives.

Traffic Police

- We see a lot of people. Most people break traffic rules. Without a helmet, without a licence, speeding and other things, even though traffic fines are levied, but there is no change in them. What our government going to decide is that if they break the traffic rules, they should be punished for a whole day in one place. That means wiping the roads, planting seedlings, watering the plants planted.
- If challans are less than 3, we will impose penalties such as cleaning the roads and raising awareness. If the same challans are more than 3 for a vehicle of that motorist, the licence will be taken. We will take both license and vehicle from them and give an acknowledgement form.
- If a vehicle is required, then 20% of the vehicle price along with the fine should be tied.
- Well, if they don't want the vehicle, which means they have to pay 15% of the cart price for the licence.

"These ideas seemed to get better and better. Yes, our government does not want to collect money or challans, we want our people to have a safe life. Assigning tasks such as germination and wiping will bring about change in our people."
A minister got up and asked
is there any rule in the motor law regarding punishing a motorist?
The home minister explained with confidence
There is currently no law relating to punishment specified in any previous motor law. We must pass this G.O. to reduce accident rates and traffic violation cases.
Conclusion: -

Protecting everyone by means of police system is a very difficult task, they are always working for our well-being and protection. To the extent that we should carry out our responsibilities with discipline, it sounds better if our care is taken care of by ourselves.

"Implementing what our cabinet ministers have proposed is somewhat difficult but not an impossible. These ideas are unique to the progress and development of our state. iIam very proud of you, you are doing your part. I will let you know the next meeting in a few days.

Thankyou, all. Saying so, I ended that meeting.

That evening I got a phone call from one of our ministers.

I was shocked to hear the news that one of our minister's children had died of malnutrition.

How careless a minister was, when it comes to a child health. At the same time, another thing came to my mind how about the health of children in rural and remote areas.

Can people in rural areas afford treatment, costing more than Rs 5 lakh?

were they getting enough food and hygenic hospitality in hospitals?

did the blood donation camps really help them in ebbing death rates?

5

HEALTH

I was shocked to hear the topic of our Health Minister presentation at the very next meeting. I did not even ask him to do homework on this topic. I feel it was my greatness to have these cabinet ministers in our party.

He started presenting his stuff.

5.1 Child care

Word Introduction: -

"Childhood is a very precious in human life. It may be in the growth of man, or it may be in learning good intellect. In the same way, health is also very important for children because at that age, the immune system starts to grow. The central government and the state governments are taking several precautions. However, children are more susceptible to the disease at an young age, when the immune system is weak and at a time when the immune system is growing. The cost of their medical care is so high that the government wants to accompany such babies."

Content Analysis: -

Some of them have already started a lot of welfare schemes for children from the central government yet state governments

1. Reproduction, Maternal, New-born, Child, Adolescence.

2. Maternal and child care agenda.

3. Integrated Child Development Sector.

all welfare programs are very useful for the child. Through government providing clean and nutritious food for children in the form of mid-day meals and more is being provided in the form of subsidy in other forms. But, these only apply to those whose annual income is less than Rs 6 lakh. Arogya Bheema is also provided in any private hospital for children up to Rs 5 lakh. our solution is , We solve any health problem for free for every child under the age of six through our government. This will ensure that, children under the age of 6 are not harmed. Insurance and Health Shree are also applicable for children above 6 years.

Conclusion: -

"Parents protect children who know nothing, but who protects parents from financial hardship. So, the goal of our government is, to fully care for children and provide them with nutritious food and medical care."

Being a part in this development, besides me, my colleagues gave consent to donate 10% from the salaries.

I would like to present another topic if chief minister agrees

I gave him permission to present another topic. Then he started medical camps.

5.2 MEDICAL/ BLOOD CAMP (Blood Donation Camps)

Word Introduction: -

"In many parts of the villages, many people suffer from illness. They go to private hospitals and government hospitals, whether they have no money, financial difficulties or some other problem. People going to a private hospital in an emergency, even if you receive better treatment at a government hospital."

Content Analysis: -

What the state government is going to decide for that is, that doctors should go to the panchayat every day and set up health camps. There, they have to provide services for free, and they have to take special care on the health issue. They need to create awareness about diet and exercise.

Then one of the ministers got up and told him, it is an old scheme which in progress and it is being implemented all over in the country.

can we find any preliminary stage in this scheme?

Says yes, for sure. Let us divide the hospitals according to the panchayat ratio. 1 hospital is required for 4 panchayats after all the calculation and house term.

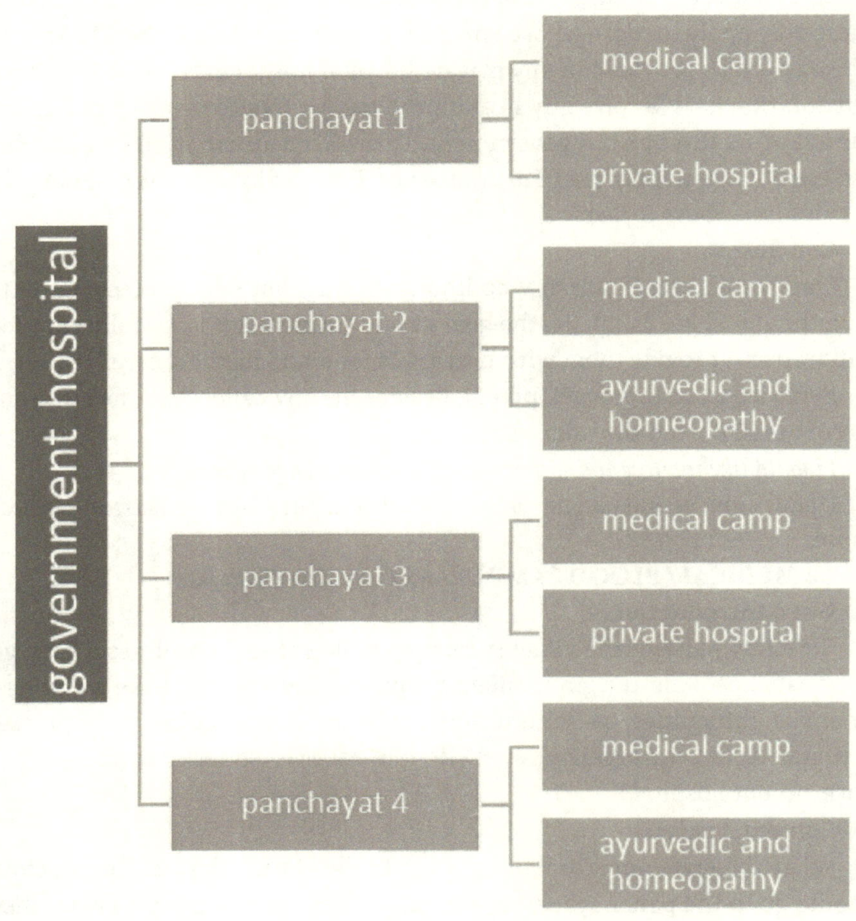

HOSPITALS IN PANCHAYAT.

Medical camps

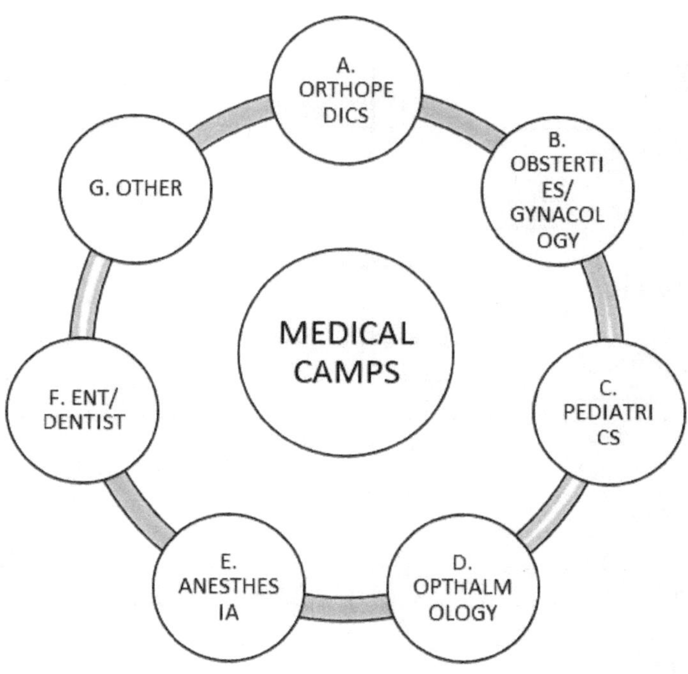
A.
ORTHOPE
DICS
B.
OBSTERTI
ES/
GYNACOL
OGY
G. OTHER
MEDICAL
CAMPS
C.
PEDIATRI
CS
F. ENT/
DENTIST
D.
OPTHALM
OLOGY
E.
ANESTHES
IA

Weeks	Panchayat 1	Panchayat 2	Panchayat 3	Panchayat 4
Monday	A (FORENOON)	C	E	G
	B(AFTERNOON)	D	F	A
Tuesday	C	E	G	B
	D	F	A	C
Wednesday	E	G	B	D
	F	A	C	E
Thursday	G	B	D	F
	A	C	E	G
Friday	B	D	F	A
	C	E	G	B
Saturday	D	F	A	C
	E	G	B	D
Sunday	F	A	C	E
	G	B	D	F

MEDICAL CAMP TIME TABLE

Awesome!!!!

But another question

"How would you place all the devices in one place?"

"The answer is, let us select 7 different places in the panchayat for each camp so that it will be easier for people to go to the specific camp, otherwise we will build a building to set up all the medical camps in one place and the doctors will follow the schedule."

Conclusion: -

Villages without medical camps are cemeteries under the house!!!!!!!!

I appreciate the words spoken by our ministers. Then another minister came and expressed his feelings.

Sir, why don't we add blood donation as we were discussing medical issues so that we could do our part in the coming days.

"When I heard about blood donation, I was reminded of the fact that my cousin died of Thalassemia. Many are also struggling with a lack of donors. This factor may be small for some of us but it was too big for those who need blood."

Word Introduction: -

"The greatest of all donations is blood donation. With a one-time blood donation, 3-4 can be saved. The same thalassemia means a lot to those who benefit because of blood. Due to lack of Blood, many lives are lost at the right time. Similarly, some are losing blood in an accident in many cases. It is our mission to protect such people."

Content Analysis: -

Blood donation Camps should be set up in every village to take blood from the people and collect it and give it to those in need. Some myths, donating blood can cause many people to become bored. All of them need to be made aware of every aspect of blood donation beyond the health benefits of donating blood. Students and Asha workers working there should take responsibility and inform everyone. Therefore, more people should be encouraged to donate blood. Benefits are available at the Government Hospital for any village from which the largest donation of blood is received.

- This means that there will be a 20 per cent deduction from the fees besides the Arogya Shree scheme.
- Many people want to donate blood, but their weight is still unable to do so due to a health problem. We recognize them as staff in the blood donation camp and present them with a certificate of appreciation once every 2 years.

Conclusion: -

"Those who guard the nerves are equal to God. It is not Caste, not religion, but blood is the only thing needed when an accident occurs. Everyone must come forward and save 4."

Yes, the views of my cabinet ministers are beyond my expectations. They are looking forward to the development of our state.

Thank you all, for taking your time and sharing your valuable ideas.

"I think you are holding a public meeting in each of your constituencies. Don't panic with people's questions, be confident that we are young people with no political experience and remember that this is our new journey. So, let them know these G.O and the laws that we are going to enforce for them. And ask them to state their problems in their daily lives. When we meet again here, we will solve

important and most useful problems and look to find solutions to them in all ways."

Thank you all......

6
EDUCATION

(1 week later)

On that day, I really felt nervous. I just thinked How people had greeted our team.

I was called on for meeting.

Hello everyone, how are you?

How have you been with people all these days? How did you spend time with our family members?

Well, to me though they gave me joy and respect and they shared their feelings with me.

I'm really happy with my teammates. Having spoken well, we began to sort out the problems facing the people in our state.

The first and foremost is education.

6.1 PLAYGROUND

Word Introduction: -

"Games have gained immense importance in human life. Although many children are passionate about games, pressure from parents or teachers make then to read. There are no playgrounds, if they want to play without pressure. The games are played to reduce stress. We are very serious about this.

Content Analysis: -

"We have been taking very unexpected decisions and actions that no one has ever expected, from the time of government formation. In the same way, now schools are also being decided in an unexpected way. Every school and college must have a playground. The school management will be given a two-month grace period. Anyone, who still does not have playgrounds as suggested by the government will be fined and given another two months to expire. The playground is still need to set up, and the college or school is besieged. Health and mental happiness are just as important as education for children. Even these educational institutions that do not have games are not allowed to run."

There are still a lot of educational institutions that are tied up and run wherever they go to the right place or on the side of the road. The government is also giving them a piece of advice as it is difficult to change them now. Playgrounds set up by the government allow students to play. But each student has to pay 10 rupees. That amount should be paid only by the College Management. No fees should be charged from students in the name of arrears. If they will not provide playground as suggested like government or if they still depend on old methodology then I will pack all these educational institutions next year, without giving any warning or intimation."

Report: -

Total schools in India = 15,00,000.

Total Panchayats in India = 2,60,000.

Schools in a Panchayat = 15,00,000 / 2,60,000 = 6.

Schools in total 20,000 panchayats = 20,000 X 6 = 1,20,000.

S.NO	schools	Percentage	Number
1.	Government	68.48	82,200.
2.	Aided	5.6	6,720.
3.	Private	22.4	26,880.
4.	Other	3.5	4,200.
5.	Total	100	1,20,000.

According to the DISE report

SCHOOLS

"40% of schools do not have playgrounds."

Total schools without playgrounds = 40/100 x 1,20,000 = 48,000.

Of the 48,000 schools, 25,000 schools were taken under private control imagine they did not have a playground. Now is the time for our government to take action.

One playground will be constructed for every 2 or 3 panchayats.

Then you want 2 playgrounds for 12 schools.

4000 playgrounds for 25,000 schools ...

Not only playgrounds but also complexes will be built on the site. The complex will have yoga, a library, study room, farmer counselling centre, medical camps, etc. all built-in in one place. Let us discuss all these in detail.

These 4000 playgrounds will be built by the government. Our policy is to give playground to every school that does not have playground to play. No fee should be charged from children for this. Only school management should have to pay Rs. 10 per child. Doing so should tie up the entire school ownership. Strict action will be taken against the complaint if he or she is tied up with children. This is done without even allowing tuition fees to be regulated.

Now, there are only 2 ways to ownership

- Build a playground.
- Pay money using government space.

As seen in the 2nd method

For example, in each school if 700 then the total population = 700 x 25,000 = 17500000

If we look at 10/- from each other, the total = 17,00,00,000/-

All ponies come to 15 crores a week.

What more surprising about this is that in India it spends 3 paise just for a person to play games. In the US, it is 22 rupees. In the UK it is 50 paise. Even in Jamaica, they are spending more money than in India, 19 paise. What a miserable situation!!!!!!!

Conclusion: -

"The ending should be to the essay but not to the game being played, not to the existing art. Games going into the business is like pushing players into darkness."

The second important thing here is NURSE.

Nurse?

I wonder, what was the relationship between a nurse and the school. I eagerly asked the Minister of Education.

And then he continued!!

6.2 NURSE (Nurse)

Word Introduction: -

"Education is just as important for children as games and health. A girl does not tell everyone the pain she is going through during the time of periods. There must be a nurse or a junior medical officer to accompany them at such times. Being a mother or sister at home can be a little daunting but a little scary even if you have friends at school."

Content Analysis: -

That is why being an Education minister, I am going to make a decision. We make it mandatory to employ an ANM or a nurse or a medical staff in every college, school and Institute of education. They have to come to school and college every day. Their salary is paid by the school management. Perform given medical-related tasks. Lessons should be taught to children about the health problems that sometimes they face. should also be taught what they know about PTSD, what females need to take care of during periods cramps, and what they need to know about medical care. Sex education should also be mentioned a few times.

The benefits of doing so

- Prostitution can still reduce and also obscene behaviour on women or Female
- They are very useful for raising awareness and warning about corona-like and catastrophic situations.
- While doing so does not alleviate much of the misery, it can also be seen as educating students from an early age without crossing boundaries and without misbehaving. The importance of sex education or many other difficulties. Let us cross them.

Conclusion: -

"It is the faculty, not the treasures, but the perceptions that need to be more on campus," he said.

What matters is not the outcome, not the position, but the environment, the way things are done."

exactly!!!!1

Our ministers are thinking very well. I, M.L. A or M.Ps should be congratulated not only but everyone working for this government.

I never imagined that an Education minister would combine both education and nursing like this. But his idea was speculative. This law should be passed as soon as possible for the betterment of the community.

We had reached our time and I had asked the Minister of Education to continue his ideas in the coming Cabinet session ...

Thank you for coming here and constantly working for the people.

That evening my daughter came up to me with a bandage on her body. I asked what had happened and she told me she slipped and Immediately, the school management took me to the hospital nearby. I was scared Daddy said my princess.

Yes, the doctors say our girl is very strong then What are you afraid of?

We will fix this as soon as possible.

So, i asked her how her friends were.

"Okay, Dad, they'were good. They were doing their part in school but one of my friends was not going to school."

Then ,I asked curiously, why?

She left our school and went to private school, but was sent home due to some financial problems.

After hearing her words, it seemed to me that there were some loopholes in the education system and tuition fees.

Therefore, it was important to analyse and advance my ideas for educating children in private and public institutions.

The result was the idea of regulating school fees. Although there was a regulation of fees in every state, I would like to move forward by amending the ongoing laws.

But this time I want to stand before our ministers to represent this situation.
(Cabinet meeting day)

"Thank you all, for coming here."

Today. I want to present the most important issues in our society. I.e., school fees.

6.3 SCHOOL FEE (Private School Fee Regulation)

Word Introduction: -

"No matter, how many children want to study hard, they end up in government school for some reason or other. Some parents enrolled their children in private schools. Higher fees are charged from those children who enrolled themselves in such a private school. Anything that comes to children through this is a total void."

Parents sweat and pay fees to support the future of their children. Private schools plunder and eat as much as they can.

Content Analysis: -

Another decision coming from the government for such people.

"A five-member committee is set up to send every five hundred schools and oversee the school's essentials, equipment, and all kinds of facilities and divide the schools into categories ABCD and classify the school in A, B, C, D category according to their equipment and facilities. That's what happens in most places up to here. But our government will charge fees depending on the category. Fees are also fixed according to their facilities. If you want to increase the fees of that private college, you should contact this committee. If all goes well, this committee will give you an increase in fees. Otherwise, 20 per cent will be deducted from the existing fee. Since basic education is very important for children, it is the responsibility of the Education Officer to ensure that there is no corruption under the supervision of this committee. One can see that the fees in the school are the same for everyone but the 1 item that is there should be used by everyone, so the fees should be decided to keep in view, everyone. They should read and understand the report and proposals made by this five-member committee, every month and make them understandable to the public. All of these are also available at help desks. Fees should also be taken care of without a high percentage. If you find that you are being taken a higher percentage of the fee, can go to the help desk and compare the fee there and the fee is charged. Be aware of problems and suggestions from the child from month to month.

Conclusion: -

"Education is not a weapon to destroy but a pen to restart. "

6.4 EDUCATION (Reading and Knowledge)

Word Introduction: -

"Most of the students we see will get good marks. Some may not get good marks. It is very difficult to Offer the same kind of job to everyone."

That is why a decision was taken on behalf of our government.

Content Analysis: -

Education system is divided into two types.

• An Academic certificate.

• Skill certificates.

That means person with good marks can come and apply for my job, as well as low marks in exams can also apply if there is a certificate of proficiency in a skill related to job. Exam can be applied anyway.

But there are some rules regarding skill: -

- Certificate Only those who have worked for more than four years are eligible for this skill certificate
- It is observed by three persons.

  - The first person is that company, may be the team leader regarding the industry or related to organisation.
  - The second is the chairman, but not the manager in this regard.
  - Third is the signature of the higher authority of the panchayat or zone area only after completing document verification.

Only after all the 3 stages, certificate or acknowledge will be issued to that candidate. The Certificate of Proficiency is as useful and valuable as that of Academic Certificate. Finally, depending on the interview conducted by the government, that is, they are interviewed separately for skills and academics and offer letter will be given based on merit of that candidate.

Conclusion: -

"Education is necessary for everyone, but it is a mistake to think that education will bring jobs and money. Education illuminates the man, as well as the work of the skilled."

6.5 MIDDAY MEALS (Lunch Plan)

Word Introduction: -

"The lunch scheme is running in many states, many districts and many places in India. This will provide free food to young children."

Content Analysis: -

The main purpose of the afternoon meal is to make sure that everyone is equal. In many places, children are not getting the food they need in terms of health, which is why many are getting sick.

There are also some types of these

- Underweight.
- Age-appropriate diet.
- Overweight.

India is trying its best to reduce malnutrition cases as expected. The good decision I am going to make from our government is that this afternoon health plan applies to the old age home as well as the orphanage. Through this, the children as well as the adults in the nearby old age home will be served meals. The main purpose of the lunch scheme of government is to provide up to one pound of rice to the people in orphanage and old age home so that everyone does not go hungry.

This means that if there are two schools in the vicinity of an old age home, tiffin and meals will come from one school in the morning, and we will arrange lunch from another school. These all vary over time. Full feedback on baby meals is taken from them. We provide biscuits, and nutritious food for the children in the evening. Sometimes, we even try to set up dry fruits. What should be the meal for adults is that some people have sugar, some people have BP, some people have a different disease, all of measures have to be taken into consideration before preparing and sent to those houses.

Conclusion: -

"Hunger cries are heard a lot in our country. I should protect and save them from hunger deaths."

After hearing my idea everyone started to express their happiness, but I was wondering what kind of way to go to implement these schemes.

And then I thanked all of you and continued my presentation.

Another important thing is the internship.

6.6 INTERNSHIP (Internships)

Word Introduction: -

"The internship is very important in college. Through it, children can learn good knowledge and good things."

Content Analysis: -

We will now. start an internship programs in the state from 11th grade to Master. The purpose of this program is to help children learn about social consciousness and social issues, along with knowledge. All those, who are doing Engineering and Degree should be split under one batch and adopt the nearby village. Since, there are many colleges, you can work with any college.

Things to do

- Educate people on issues related to Swachh Bharat.
- make sure Villagers should get involved in Swachh Bharat.
- Water use and precautions to be taken.

- Students should be made aware of everything they know by sharing it with them.
- Adopt a village and strive to achieve 100% literacy. In this way, our state will be 100% literate like Kerala.
- It is the responsibility of the students to fill in the blank forms, the small things and the simple things, the welfare schemes from the Central Government and the new things and to say things that are sure to go and be understood.
- Night classes can also be started as daytime farming is sufficient for the farmers, so the boys can watch the class.

All of you will be given an internship certificate on behalf of VRO. Benefits are these can be used for government jobs. We will give more opportunities in government jobs to all those who work for the betterment of the villages for the most of the years.

Some rules in this regard: -

- Go to the village at least 2 times a week and arrange classes there as pre-arranged by VRO Garu.
- Educate them with the knowledge about horticulture, agriculture etc. on how to grow trees related to agriculture what sort of chemicals should be used for the benefit of all. Some people, like their countryside as a guide for those who come to the tourist area to understand the uniqueness of the town, so to speak.
- An internship Certificate will be given to the students on behalf of the Government.

Conclusion: -

"Education should not end with you, life should start with new ones. Every student must help and impart knowledge to their country and city."

Last important in this sector is free coaching services.

6.7 FREE COACHING

Word Introduction: -

"Many students and individuals in the state want to become soldiers or policemen and serve our country and or state. But, due to their financial difficulties, they are not able to go to the intended place due to lack of any incentive. "

The state government wants to help them.

Content Analysis: -

We will train those, who want to become police or soldiers in advance and make it easy for them to reach their destination concerning the police and the army for free. This is done completely free of charge for every student.

We teach you all the education a student needed to become a policeman completely free of charge. This only applies to those under 25 years and those will have to pay a fee after 25. Physical fitness can be acquired and the equipment and tutor required for it will be provided by the government.

But the small request from them is that if they get a job tomorrow, they can help with the maintenance of the school where they are studying with 1000 rupees. This can lead to the joy of how many people we are giving and helping in the future. Every month, those who are policemen for the state government or any work related to the centre are deducted Rs.1000 or Rs.1500 from their salary and sent directly to the coaching centre which is useful to them so every month. The country must be protected from corruption. This is the decision that is going to be taken by our government.

Many people are in a situation where they cannot read and the quest to help the country. This step of ours is for them.

A doubt in everyone, Will jobs come to everyone who comes to coaching? That. Wouldn't you be happy if you got a good job if this was not a job ...?

Conclusion: -

"How good it would be, if there was a tax on education in the country too!! Taxation in the sense not about making money; it was about sharing knowledge."

I never imagined these meetings would be so interesting. I felt really happy. Now it is time to implement the laws passed in this Cabinet meeting. now, its time to call day of. saying so, I ended meeting.

The next day I was called to watch the news, in which, opponents criticized that we were not producing money or money aspected. They started blaming us for not being in a position to make money. But what I do know is that we started our new journey ,with good ideas ,even though it was a difficult task. But they did not understand what they were looking for. So, I called the opposition leaders for an all-party meeting. So, I started asking them questions. After a healthy discussion, we came up with new ideas. Really, thank the Opposition and the leaders of other parties for participating in this discussion. Those ideas could really benefit us and the people a lot.

Most ideas were based entirely on the WEALTH FROM WASTE concept.

Some ideas were listed below.

7

ENVIRONMENT

7.1 ELECTRICITY (Electricity)
Word Introduction: -

"Electricity should be used very carefully, either in our state or in our country. We see that in many places or many districts most of the resources are being wasted by misusing electricity. This can lead to financial difficulties. Here comes the actual power crisis when coal stored in power plants started depleting. Although solar panels are already in use. In many parts of the country, they do not reach every home. Because of some problems like cost, reliability and duration."

Content Analysis: -

Therefore, the decision taken by our government is to reduce the use of electricity by replacing light bulbs and street lights with LEDs from small houses to large houses in the state. This is because, the yellow light bulbs used so far in the country, state and district emit a lot of heat. This causes a lot of danger to the surroundings and to catch. The crisis will be exacerbated in the coming days by the decrease the use of yellow incandescent light bulbs. So, the government will make LED bulbs completely free and useful to all.

Even though, central government and previous state governments followed and implemented this idea, but only 80% people in our country using LED bulbs. Not only in our state, we found large number of normal incandescent bulbs in many rural areas in other states. But in our state, it seemed bit higher than expected. So, we came with this idea.

S. No	INCANDESCENT	Equivalent HALOGEN	LED
1.	40	28	6
2.	60	45	11
3.	75	56	15
4.	100	80	24
life	1,000 hours	10,000hours	20-30,000 hours

BULBS

In this way, LED bulbs consume less power and burn out for a long time. This can also reduce the electricity bill. In addition, light pollution can also be reduced.

Conclusion: -

"No other creature should be pushed into darkness and confusion; we are here to live and we should let other creatures to live. The world is not just about living people, it's about birds and other living things."

7.2 RAILWAY (Power consumption in train)

Word Introduction: -

We travel by train at some point in life. As you can see, tube lights are used on the train even in the morning. This causes a lot of damage. As a Chief Minister I cannot decide on this matter because the railway station falls under the purview of central government but let us see how the damage is done.

Content Analysis: -

S. no	Types of tube lights	thickness	watts
1.	T5	Very thin	28
2.	T8	thin	36
3.	T12	normal	40

BULB THICKNESS

According to thickness, 36 watts are used in a train. As you can see, tube lights are not required from 7 AM to 5 PM. I.e., a total of 10 hours

1KWH is when a 100-watt bulb is used for 10 hours.

1KWH = 1unit

36 watts x 10 = 360 watthour = 0.36 KWH.

There are a total of 15 tube lights in a bogie and 24 bogies per train.

If 4 (engine, 2 AC, 1 last bogie) are removed, for example, there will now be a total of 20 bogies.

Tube lights on the whole train = 15X 2 = 300.

Total power = 300X 36x 10 = 108000WH, = 108KWH

Total trains in India are 12617 passengers, 7421 goods

Total power = 12617 x 108 = 13,62,636kwh

1 unit = 6 rupees (example)

Per day = 13,62,636 x 6 = 84,00,000/-

Per year = 365X 84,00,000 = 308cr.

Conclusion: -

"Water alone is not equal to Lakshmi and money, all the Panchabhutas are equal to money."

One day, we will face a crisis if we do not reduce our electricity consumption.

7.3 DAY CYCLE: -

Word Introduction: -

"Protecting this environment is the responsibility of all of us. The hardships that can be encountered can be imagined, but disasters cannot be anticipated in advance. The more we respect the environment, the better we were taken care of it."

Content Analysis: -

Our government strives to protect the environment. As part of that, the company, the industry institution and the employer must leave all cars and bikes at least once a week and comes on a bicycle, on a charging scooter and a government-provided bus, from any small industry to large. This can reduce environmental pollution. Even though it is difficult to go this route at least two days a week, we still have to work hard for our environment. Government buses or CNG autos or charging scooters or bicycles can be used during those two days. This can greatly reduce the amount of pollution. Those days will be seen below Environment Day. The office on that day starts a little late and will end a little sooner. This also applies to government offices and private offices.

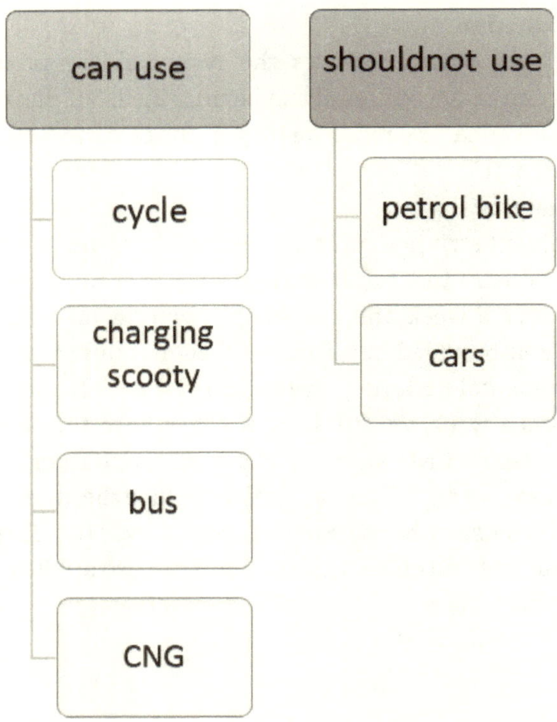

CAN AND CAN'T USE

The government has to protect the environment, to create awareness among the people and to prepare them for the coming hardships and disasters, even if they are financially damaged by the low consumption of petrol.

Conclusion: -

"Don't take environment for granted."

7.4 PLASTIC:

Word Introduction: -

"It is very important to protect the environment. Pollution of the environment or the earth is mostly caused by plastics. But we are using plastic as one of our essentials. Banning plastic all at once is very dangerous and very difficult economically. Such plastic materials, take a long time to meet in the ground. This changes the essence of the earth or the structure of the earth. The less we use and recycle such plastic, the better will be the conditions."

Content Analysis: -

It's hard to ban once in a while, so you've needed to make good toys out of that material, make a dustbin underneath and make it look like a sitting bench, and tie people up with good buildings or tourist spots to lure them out. Having an awareness of them can greatly reduce problems.

The decision we are taking through our government

Many people would be eager to see the endangered species of animals and birds made of plastic, built statues of our freedom fighters and placed in parks and for tourist attractions.

Courses in this regard are also offered in every school and college.

Benefits: -

- Can reduce land pollution.
- Can reduce the use of plastic.
- Plastic can be recycled and used to make new items.
- A variety of plastic rubbish cans, attractive toys, sculptures and benches are being constructed and designed to attract people.
- Anything overused is useless. Find a substitute for plastic.
- RRRR should be used.

Conclusion: -

"Plastic should be a help to our hands but not a threat to the earth!!!!!!

7.5 SOLAR PANELS (Environment)

Introduction: -

We have resources in our country and in our state, we are not utilizing them properly. We are also wasting existing resources. This will one day lead to a resource crisis.

Content Analysis: -

"Another law, that the government is going to take is to conserve the resources at the same time we have to reduce electricity. During the summer, only up to 500 units of electricity are supplied per month to each residential home in the municipality, city and town."

Flats and commercial buildings up to 1000 units can only be given by the government. We will discuss the industries in advance and plan the unit as per the requirements. Naturally, no more than 500 units can be used for residential buildings. Even if more than 500 units are used, they must install solar panels. This calculation varies from season to season. This unit is likely to grow during the rainy season. In winter and monsoon, there are no boundaries from the Government as usual. This has to be done to some extent during the summer. The flat with a height of more than G + 2 have to install solar panels. Due to the high rate of solar panels, many people do not like them. But we will see to it that those who bring and use solar panels are subsidized by the government. For those who install solar panels, the unit will be reduced by Rs 2, which is Rs 5 per unit, to Rs 3 only. Through it, a company that makes solar panels will see the law set up in our state and create many jobs.

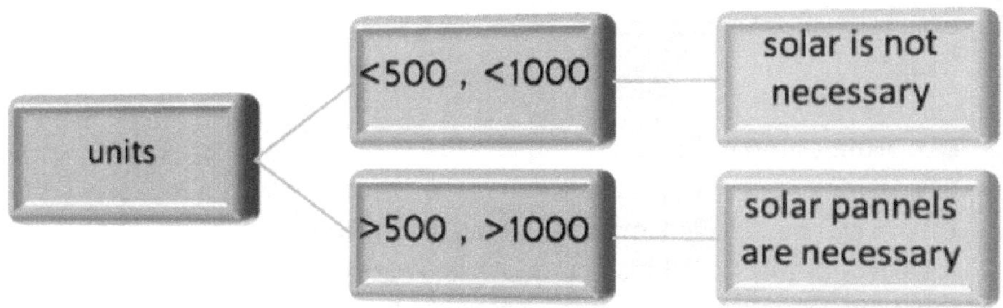

UNITS

It can also save a lot of resources. They can use those resources well in the future. For the farmers in the village, it is 300 to 500 units without any interruption as usual.

Conclusion:

It is a difficult task for both caregivers to find happiness (light) and love (heat) and to transform differently."

I think we only have a 3 to 4 weeks deadline for assembly meetings. Before the Assembly sessions, I asked my Cabinet and all the MLAs to present their ideas in a multifaceted manner.

Ready to counter everything that the opponent masters put.

Although we made a lot of decisions, I went through the last public meetings because I felt that these meetings needed an extra dose. In them, I found some interesting things. So, I ordered all my M.L.A and M.L.C to submit these and the things left before me. They did as I said.

The topic they presented at the next cabinet session was about the structural development of villages and some infrastructure.

An MLA from our state stood up and started giving a presentation.

He greeted; Sir I am proud to be a part of this party sir. I know you will not like some of my highlights in this presentation, but I've really going to try my part and present it to you.

We all know that infrastructure plays a major role in our society and it is important to develop them. Our family also facedsome problems when I moved to certain parts of our state. All of these are listed in front of you. I started working on those issues. I want everyone to come forward and correct me if there are mistakes in my thoughts.

8

INFRASTRUCTURE

8.1 VILLAGE (Village)

Word Introduction: -

"There are many villages in our state. The countryside is the backbone of the country. So, we should develop with no limits. So, as a part this we are going to redesign every village in our state. The idea is, to run a complex. In that complex We will set up hospitals, concerts, theatres, banks, agriculture, support centres, yoga centres, libraries, gymnasiums and cold storage centres and make them accessible to everyone. For this, up to 100 rupees is taken from each family in each village once a month. We see all of this working 24 hours a day. We will try to save these hundred rupees for maintenance and for utilizing the available resources as well as salaries."

As we all know that village mainly consists of green jungle, we should not make it as a concrete jungle. Complex means running all the things and necessities in a single point so large amount of land can be saved for agriculture.

So, that we are setting up education knowledge and health for the people without any hassle. Doubts related to agriculture are overseen, yoga centres, library excise, all of which are handled by government school teachers and Pts.' The staff is supportive of everyone who want to educated, both children and adults, and tells them to share their knowledge without embarrassment. A reading room will also be set up next to the library so that we can see each subject as told by each teacher once a day for a week. The greatness given by literacy is that we make it seem like everything can be put to good use by everyone from small children to adults without any hassle.

The building contract will be awarded to private companies.

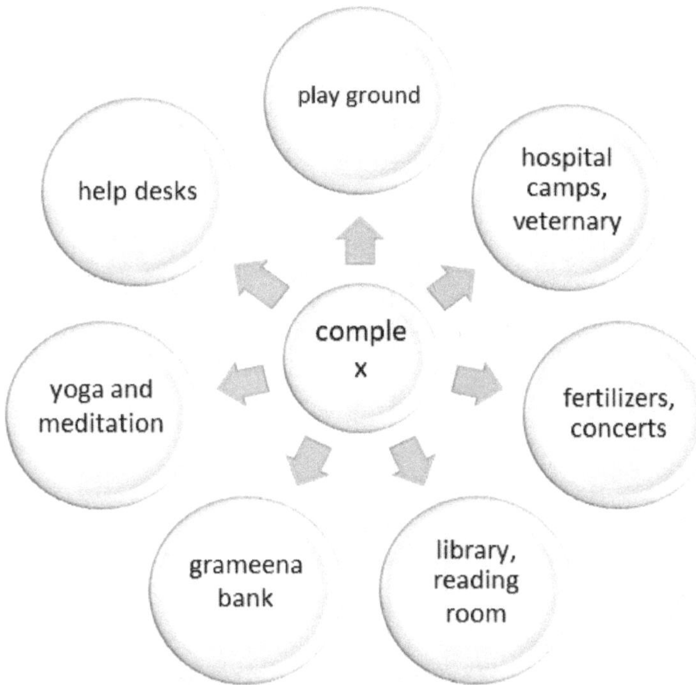

Content Analysis: -
8.2 GOVERNMENT LIBRARY (Government Library)

Already the government is making some very sensational decisions. Now, it is the responsibility of the government to divide the districts under each panchayat and to set up a playground for each of the two panchayats, along with a park, a library and reading rooms, and a yoga complex under one complex. For every 2 months, the books will be interchanged from 1 panchayat to another. In this way we can attract readers to library. In this way, we can also make yoga useful for the adults so that the children do not have to go anywhere to play and the students are not inconvenienced and financially distressed. The same flat will be taken every two months at the rate of 200 per family.

A good teacher will be set up to train all these through the government. Through this, we are ready to reduce the unemployment problem for those in that place and serve them more if more tax comes to that panchayat than expected.

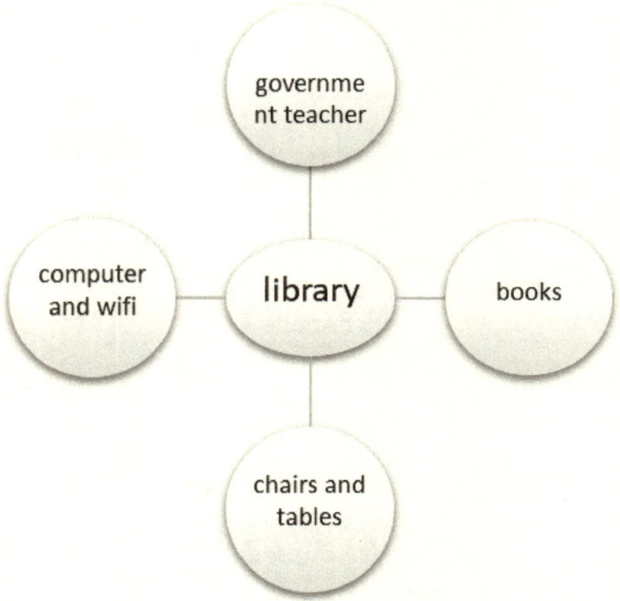

LIBRARY REQUIREMENTS

S. no	Area	cost
1.	panchayat	100
2.	municipality	200

COST/ AREA

8.3 HUTS (cottage)

"On most roads either, we do not see the minimum facilities on most roads concerning national highways and state highways. There are no trees to stand on in summer. During the monsoon season, the culprit gets wet if he has to go home. It is like a kind of stand for the government to get out and stay without any trouble for such people, and public toilets will be set up. All of this work entirely on solar panels. The government will step in to ensure that the people reach their destination with full protection without any hassle. It also has an SMS set up so that in case of an accident to anyone, if anyone is in trouble, they should immediately send a message to their nearest home. The information is sent to their houses so that they can see without any trouble, and the camera also works. All activities there are fully supervised by the authorities. SOS is used not only for messaging but also for shade, charger and other requirements through the cottage. A charger point will also be set up. We have set up such huts right here at the tollgates where a fee of Rs 10 to Rs 15 will be charged. The bar code paper with the fee so charged in a tollgate. so that, passengers can enter through a sensor scanner near the cottage. This is because, so many people use it unnecessarily.

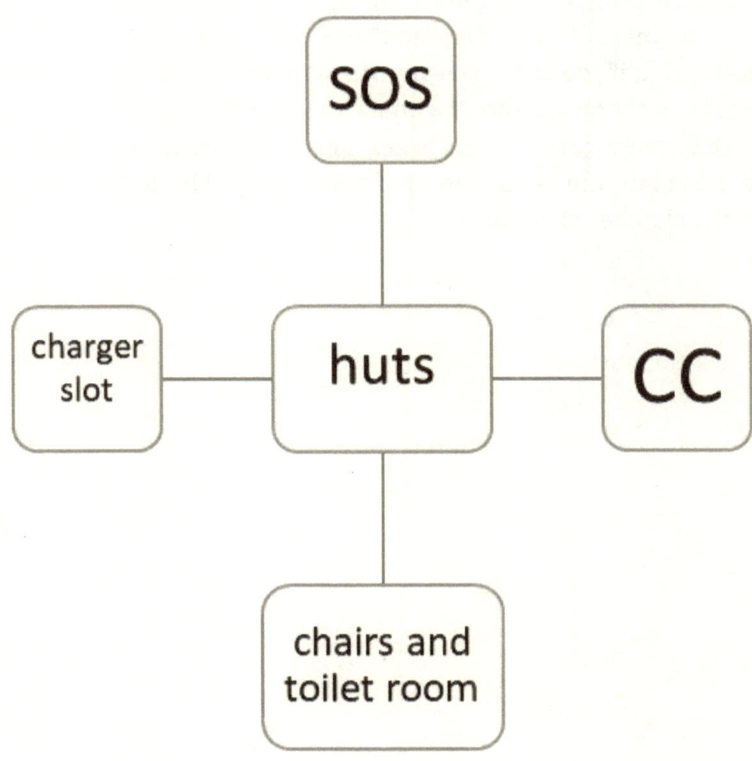

HUTS REQUIREMENTS

8.4 PUBLIC TOILET

"We see that either on the road or on the highway, in many places women do not have as much freedom as men to defecate and use the toilet. In many places, women have to work very hard to get rid of it. Although there are public toilets in every petrol bunk without any hassle for such people, some of them we do not see in the petrol bunk on some highways. It will be very embarrassing for them. Another important decision being taken by the government for such people is to set up one public toilet per kilometre. This is how we say in advance that girls or boys everywhere will do it without any trouble. The fee for this is to keep the toilets clean.

A card will be issued to those who use public toilets. Those cards are up to thirty digits long. If they have to go to the restroom on the way there, the maintainer will put a stamp on the card with the name and location of the public toilet and send it inside. Similarly, wherever there are public toilets everywhere, a person using public toilets will have a stamp on the card. If the card amount is filled in this way, then 5 bus trips in that district are free. This means that if you can travel anywhere in the district by bus after filling up, there is no charge for showing that card. Only 50km free.

For this, there are 5 more boxes under 30 which are filled with a conductor. main aim is to raise awareness on public toilets and protect against the clutches of diseases.

Details				
1. stamp	2	3	4	5
6	7	8	9	10
11	12	13	14	15
16	17	18	19	20
21	22	23	24	25
26	27	28	29	30
1. Conductor sign	2.	3	4	5

PUBLIC TOILETS

8.5 GOVERNMENT RESTAURANT (Government Restaurant)

"Government should start restaurants and canteens. No one in our state should suffer without rice, so our government has taken steps to provide three meals a day for everyone. A Government Canteen will be started at a Radius every 20 kilometres. Meals will be provided for those who are travelling. Meals at a government-run restaurant are provided at a lower rate than outside restaurants, and care must be taken to ensure that each person eats as much as he or she wants. The advantage of this is that people will not starve and can use the rice grain that has been damaged by the rains or any other disaster. As the value of the grain decreases over time, the grain is served in a canteen or restaurant set up by the government, using a grain of rice. The grain is inspected by a horticulture and agriculture specialist to find out if there are any problems if they feel this grain and meal and everything is safe then it will be sent to restaurants then familiar meals and food will be served in the morning, afternoon and evening. The meal is sometimes sent to government-run orphanages and nursing homes. Our goal is to see people without any starvation."

8.6 HUMAN EXCRETA

"A plant should be established that produces organic matter and chemicals from man's excrement to the crop.

Most of the village crops we see are farmed using cow and buffalo manure. Human excreta should not be used as a pesticide as it contains certain chemicals that can only be used for harvesting after they have been removed. There are a few problems with using it directly. A good crop can be harvested if it is provided to the crop through this type of preparation. Since most of the public toilets are being set up as not every house can be collected separately, human excrement through them is to go directly to the plant and remove the contaminants in the excrement there and use it as per the crop requirements.

It is also known as Night Soil in another language. This is not new to you in our country, but most of us are suffering due to a lack of equipment and technology. There are only 130 of these plants in our country. It is our goal to increase in our state as well."

8.7 WATER TREATMENT PLANT

As discussed earlier a good sump tank will be maintained in every village or every panchayat as well as in every village but also near every pond a water treatment plant will be maintained. This will provide safe drinking water to the people without any hassle. Many people suffer from health problems due to drinking contaminated water everywhere. Although water is free, many are unable to provide the minimum safe freshwater. Water is coming in the same way for the municipality and differently for the panchayats. In the same villages, there will be water containing a combination of excrement and sewage. Together with all these, various diseases are coming to the people of the village. So, we will provide free fresh water and safe water to the people in the village. We will charge a maintenance charge of up to Rs 200 per family as mentioned earlier. Our goal is to keep people healthy through this. It is very difficult to build a large water treatment plant at once, so we can tailor the water treatment to suit the conditions using two types of process namely slow sand process and quicksand process and complete it with less money without lowering water standards. We can also use reverse osmosis process.

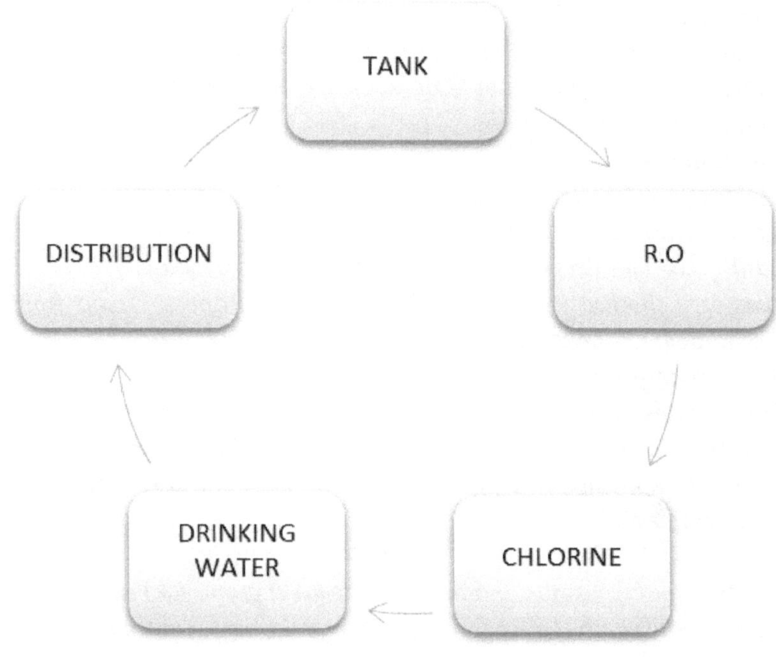

WATER PROCESS

8.8 SKILL DEVELOPMENT (Talent)

Most people in our state, our country or our district have awareness and talent on many things in life. It is very difficult to bring everyone on the same path. Many in our state are suffering from a lack of proper reception despite their talents. Under the great opportunity for all of them, the government will set up programs five to six times a month to bring out the great things and talents in them and give them a better future. We will make a separate course-like education for other countries or them if necessary and make it useful for them.

So, we will give scholarships through the Government to any talented person if required. We will do our best to support their progress. Most of them draw drawings. They have a lot of habits and grip, but there are very few who work for their prosperity, about those in most states. So, we put all the people who draw together and give them good training and give them all a job in the tourist area and the park and in various places and earn money. Salaries are also paid only for work done. In this way, the population of the tourist area can grow as well as the treasury can be filled, and they can also be shown to be open to life.

The countryside must be protected as well as light into their lives. Lack of education does not make villages prosperous. We need to see that they have good welfare and development.

Conclusion: -

"It is not good to turn villages into yards and sell them as villages. It will change the future of the country."

Thank you all for listening attentively to what I have to say.

I was very shocked when I heard these problems and solutions from him. What he said was happening in our society.

I had to congratulate him.

We had made some laws regarding these issues. At the next meeting, I told my members that I was going to present some more ideas. I was also told that there would be a kitchen meeting that day. So, I'm going to perform in front of important people and people.

(That day)

Leaders of the Opposition, thank you to the great people for being here.

I told them things that were going and laws from the beginning and they were really satisfied with our government. Some also raise questions such as how our government balances the budget.

I replied to them, if we want to grow a plant, we must first water that plant. If we think that giving water reduces the amount of water, our thinking is different.

Eventually, I began to demonstrate the rest of the problems that exist in our community.

9

OTHER

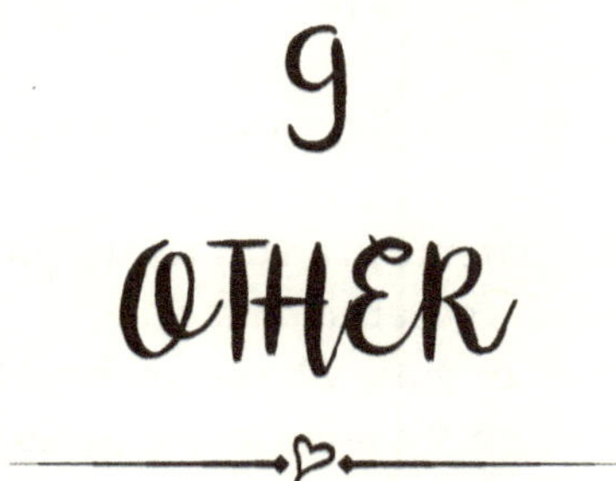

9.1 ORPHANAGE AND OLD AGE HOMES

Word Introduction: -

Every day I take charge as Chief Minister, I live a great life and with inspiring ideas. I always strive to accompany people in every category and reassure them. In such a case, I got a call one morning from someone outside.

Hello,

One person lamented and said that everyone in our house was an orphan in an orphanage.

he convey me that they wanted to spend time with children and family, but we were a burden to them.

After discussing this family matter with them, our teeth were blown out earlier than expected. Weight loss will be followed by fatigue because of constant tiredness.

Please, let me beg you to do something.

As soon as I heard that, I sent word to everyone that there was a cabinet meeting.

Everyone came.

I fully explained what had happened.

Everyone thought with great skill and came up with a good idea.

Content Analysis: -

"There are many orphanages and old age homes in the country. There are also many old age homes and orphanages in our state. Some are self-established, but some are government-run.

What we are going to do now is take over all the orphanages and old age homes in the government.

Let us first talk about things related to old age home.

- Those, who leave their parents in an orphanage home do not receive any welfare schemes from the government.
- Old age homes are only for those who do not have family members, those whose family is elsewhere for some unavoidable reason and those who are struggling with disabilities and unable to look after their parents.
- I am going to bring in a rule called Granny Adoption through which is anyone adopts an adult in an old age home they will get welfare schemes, reservations and other opportunities from the state government irrespective of caste. Government officials come one day each month to inquire about their well-being.
- One or two warnings if the adoptive parent says that the elderly are not better than the nursing home, either in the adoption or in the ashram, then the adoption will start cutting welfare schemes.
- Funds for a government-run old age home can be obtained from either the public or the government.
- If someone, who does not want welfare schemes and leaves their children and the elderly in an orphanage or an old age home, imposing a 30 to 40 per cent cut deduction in their professional salary.
- If someone begs though having family members. They will not get any welfare scheme and other facilities in their family, and they will also be imprisoned for two months.

Let's talk about the orphanage: -

- Children under 12 who do not have parents are perceived as orphans and placed in an orphanage.
- Young children who are beggars are considered orphans and are placed in an orphanage. Strict action will be taken against the parents if they beg even if they have parents.
- They should be fully educated up to the age of 16 years.

Orphanage and old age homes.
Report: -

4% of our Indian population are orphans.

There are 3 crore orphanages in India.

Total Panchayats in India = 2,60,000.

Every panchayat has orphans = 3,00,00,000 / 2,60,000 = 11.

Orphans in 20,000 panchayats = 20,000 x 11 = 2,20,000.

Old age home-

There are 750 ashrams in India.

According to Google, there are up to 250 old age homes in Andhra Pradesh alone.

The ratio for the elderly and nursing homes is 1: 125.

Take Andhra Pradesh for example, the total number of elderly people in Andhra Pradesh = 250x125 = 31,250.

Total number of orphanages and waste shelters combined

= 2,20,000 + 31,250 = 2,51,250.

60% of the elderly resort to old age homes due to family quarrels and psychological violence alone. That is, the total = 31250 60/100 = 18,750.

The rest = 31250 - 18750 = 12500.

Desired Ashrams = 12500/125 = 100.

The number of ashrams now in Andhra Pradesh will be reduced from 250 to 100.

Orphanages: -

Total if at the rate of 150 in each orphanage

= 2,00,000 / 150 = 1400

If the rest of the old age homes are converted under the orphanage, the rest = 1400-150 = 1250.

Prerequisites: -

Orphanages

The most important of them is desirable

- Food
- Clothes
- Read
- Other Equipment (Beds, Chairs)

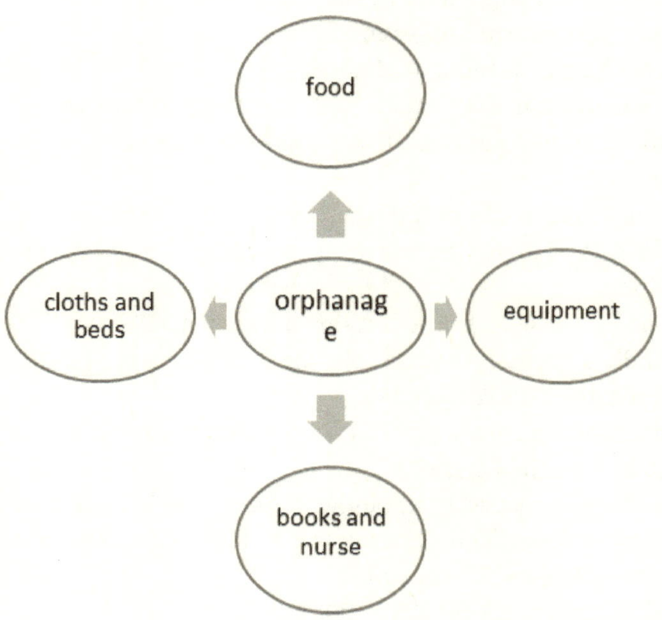

ORPHANAGE REQUIREMENTS

#Government for children in orphanages
Provides free education, so they will also be given a free uniform.
The government provided 1200 per month, for their clothes and other necessities.
Free treatment at any hospital, regardless of their health status.
2,00,000 and the total cost is = 1200 x 2,00,000. = 24 crores.
Desired Staff = 1250x 3 = 3750.
Their salary (10 thousand per person) = 3750 x 30,000 = 12 crores.
For other needs = 3 crores.
The total cost of the orphanage = 15 crore + 24 crore = 39 crores.
Old age home
Facilities required for an old age home

- Clothes
- Meal
- 1 doctor and nurse
- Other requirements

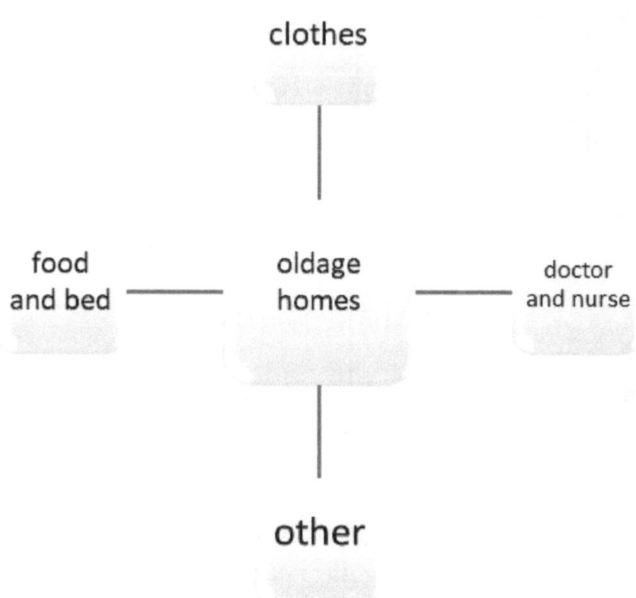

OLDAGE HOME REQUIREMENTS

100 Waste Ashram Staff = 100x 3 = 300.
Salary = 300 x 30000 = 90,00,000 = 1 crore.
Money given to the elderly 1500 per month = 1250 x 1500 = 2 crores.
Total = 3 crores.
The total cost of the old age home and the orphanage is 49 + 3 = 43 crores.
Their meal comes every day from the canteen set up by the government.
Evening nutritious food (dry fruits, biscuits, milk) is also given to the elderly and young children in the evening.
Provide them with the money they have for the beds and chairs they need.
Their salaries vary depending on the funds.

S.n	details	%
1.	Working staff	30
2.	For items (buckets, blankets)	25
3.	Facilities	25
4.	Clothes	20

FUNDS SEGGREGATION.

We need to help, support and protect orphans who have nothing. Those who distance themselves from those who look for assets should be severely punished.

Conclusion: -

"There seems to be a measure of aid and humanity in the country, so orphanages and shelters are growing exponentially."

9.2 WATER AND GAS METERS (Water and Gas)

Word Introduction and Analysis:

"People should be made aware of gas meters and water meters. Through the gas meter, we can use only the quantity of gas that we need for the most part. Very useful when needed. Fire hazards can be reduced. From time to time, we can estimate the amount of gas we use and increase or decrease it for the next month or so. Our government is looking at launching gas meters in the countryside as most of the people in the village use wood stoves as there is no protection for the environment as this is detrimental to health as most of the people in the village are not very aware of gas as it is the only way to reduce the risk of accidents. Care should be taken not to cause any inconvenience to the crops when setting up the gas metal."

Water meters: -

Water is very useful, but most people waste water. Such is the need to ensure that a Water meter is set up for every home now. This allows you to know how much water is being used and how much tax can be levied on the public. Sump tanks should be set up in a good place in every village. It should be set up 1 per panchayat when it comes to town it is 2. The water in this volume is useful during such summer times, as most of the water evaporates during the summer.

We can also add sensors to the water meters to reduce water wastage.

Conclusion: -

If you waste water, you will go to another world without becoming old!!!!!

"The whole earth is filled with air, including you. Hand in hand with the wind will make you proud, otherwise, you will be thrown into the abyss. "

9.3 NATIVE PRODUCTS

Introduction: -

Most of the people in India have access to necessities and goods. Some goods are produced only from other countries and states. They are not available in our country. The technology in our country is not at the expected level due to illiteracy. Due to the large population of our country, we are relying on different countries to provide our people with the necessities that are increasing as the needs of each increase. In a way, it's a good thing, but it does a lot of damage, especially to the most important indigenous goods traders. As we become more and more dependent on other countries, we are reducing our expertise. This is not a good sign. In a way, it will take a toll on the economy. The domestic market provides a livelihood for many. Many people in India or the state are skilled in many things but due to the prevailing rates in the domestic market, they are not able to sell them at the right price, so they are profiting by porting them to other states and countries.

Content Analysis: -

The decision we are going to take from our government is to increase the value of the domestic market.

In a few places in the district of the state, we will select the most non-damaging places and see to it that the traders sell only the indigenous items, ranging from the razor needle used for a month to the larger item. Not all goods are made in one place, so goods from district to district should be moved to wherever in the domestic market and delivered to the people without any hassle. Even so, owning one is still beyond the reach of the average person.

Through this, the expansion of the domestic market can be enhanced. People can look for items that are not found in the market without bothering. But it has to be said that it is an adventure to have every item made in the homeland in one place. So there is a chance of losses, so some backup plans should be put in place to minimize the risks. Where domestic goods are manufactured and sold in a market, we will take steps to reduce the subsidy and sales tax by the Government as the State Government reduces the GST coverage.

If the production and popularity of domestic goods increase, we will expand elsewhere and similarly expand in the domestic market.

The benefits of this

- Indigenous expansion takes place.
- Livelihood for many.
- The opposite can be seen as less dependent on other states but other countries.
- Hand loom Textiles Handicrafts, Indigenous Experience, Indigenous Occupation In many ways, our state can be said to be all-encompassing.
- Many good industries can be set up and many of them can be given jobs.

The risks involved

- Not every item can be found in one place, so shipping goods from one place to another can make the item price a bit higher.

- Black marketing takes place in many places like in the domestic market which means people bring goods from the path.
- Losses should be reported from time to time as there is a possibility of losses.

Responsibilities to be taken

- Talk to the Centre in advance and explain the idea of domestic markets to them and ask them to come forward to help in case of any major loss.
- Sometimes we cannot find what we need in hard-earned domestic goods.
- We hope that the greatness of the indigenous goods will make them very successful by making people understand the great things in them as they are understood.
- Government will set up marts as a backup plan. If the required good is not available in indigenous. People can go to market yards setup by governmet.

Conclusion: -

"People start new arts and new ideas only when they realize the importance of the indigenous object. Whenever a man begins to think, that is the first step to victory. "

9.4 PAINTING

Word Introduction: -

"Every district in the state should also have a bridal feast for those who see how clean it is. Therefore, the roads in each district zone and each panchayat should be painted. It should be painted on the walls on both sides and shown very artistically. This method is not new. We see their painting on the walls of many highways and subways. Our goal is to set up the same painting everywhere."

Content Analysis: -

The main purpose of the painting is to print on the walls all the important things said by great scientists, leaders and warriors.

We also print awareness pictures. Through it, we create awareness among people from all walks of life.

Although this tradition has existed before, it is not everywhere. But this will cost some money to the state treasury. More money has to be spent either on painting or by those who work, but for some reason like this. The main decision that our state government is going to take is that we want to put up a painting competition on the walls in every district and every zone in the state. The competition is held every two months and participants are given a Government Certificate. The winners of the competition will be given a cash prize of 10,000 to 15000. The competition is judged by painters and dignitaries from across the region. Marks will be added depending on the wall painting and the first winner will be announced. Seen in this way, the cost is also reduced over the fact that in many parts of our state, they cause a great deal of feasting.

Note: -

- These painters or artists should not use any graffiti. The painting should not be placed where there are signal boards and information boards.

- Application for these can be made online. Can be done offline, either.
- We are giving this kind of vivo thinking that they can participate in the competition for free and show off their talents without any fee.
- The three-time winners will receive free training on design and related to art education from the government. Reimbursement will be given for pursuing painting related education in other countries and other states, as well as in our state.

Conclusion: -

"Drawing to excite our minds is no small matter. drawing alone can change the world."

9.5 DRIVING

Word Introduction and Analysis: -

Free driving training, tailoring, handicraft techniques and self-defence classes.

Although many women are very talented, they cannot find the time to do things at home but in raising and caring for children, no matter how hard they try. Until then, depending on the husband's income, once the children grow up, they will have a hard time earning enough. For the expansion of indigenous goods, we will see to it that all those who are involved in the manufacture of indigenous goods on hand loom are well-practised and enhance the development of the country state along with their development of new technologies and techniques.

Conclusion: -

" get addicted to your art, to the work you want to do, it will show you the best ways."

"There is only one woman who can change the head of a family. Tell me if her thoughts are wrong.

9.6 ALCOHOL (Liquor Policy)

Word Introduction: -

"Many in our state are becoming addicted to alcohol. Committing domestic violence, theft and endangering their lives and health. Such people are once addicted to alcohol, but it is very difficult to discipline them. Once the alcohol is lifted all of sudden, it becomes mentally disturbed and becomes a variety."

This government is totally against alcohol but will change it, so, we are bringing in a new liquor policy through which only two to two and a half litres per person will be sold per month. This is how a card is given in ration stores, where the card contains the person's name and some numbers related to the two and a half litres but all the numbers. By giving a person the opportunity to drink only 2 to two and a half litres. There is also the possibility of taking the decision of the people there and reducing it even further. But many are sceptical that we even have a suggestion on whether the black pot will happen if the card is given to non-drinkers. When going to the ration shop and picking up a card regarding alcohol, person has to show their names, addresses and proof of age. After you register, the head of the house or the woman in our house will call the adults and find out. If they think it's okay for them or our children or our siblings or adults to say they've been drinking then the card will be issued every month or else we will cancel the card which in many places will be beneficial to those who have harmed their health as well as abstain from alcohol.

The income of the state has been greatly reduced but still the welfare and future of the people are important to us. I will make sure that the alcohol card is not tampered with.

Every month of the year the liquor merchants do the same and lift what happens to the liquor and send it to the government office.

Content Analysis: -

Before analysing alcohol, let us know the details of alcohol as before.

S.no	name	ml
1	quarter	180
2	half	375
3	full	750

11% of the total population in India consumes alcohol.

S. no	Sex	Units/ week
1	male	21
2	woman	14

ALCOHOL

one unit = 25 ml

Thus, the male consumes 3 units of alcohol per day which is 3 x 25 = 75 ml

30 x75 = 2250ml = 2.250l per month

In the same way, a woman consumes 2 units of alcohol per day i.e., 2 x 25 = 50 ml

30 x 50 = 1500 ml = 1.5 ml per month

Here are how the cards are issued, but the population of our state is divided into two types.

A family is given 2 alcohol cards at the rate of one card per person

If any family needs more than two cards, they will be deducted from the pro-government welfare schemes. The card will be issued. Black marketing is more likely to happen to cardholders this way. Before going to the Manual office to detain them they have to fill the Google form asking for the name, age, proof and some details and as soon as it is done a paper will come, and they will have to go to the Mandal office with the favour. Thus, only one card per person Will is given.

That card only works for one month, and you have to pick up another card in another month.

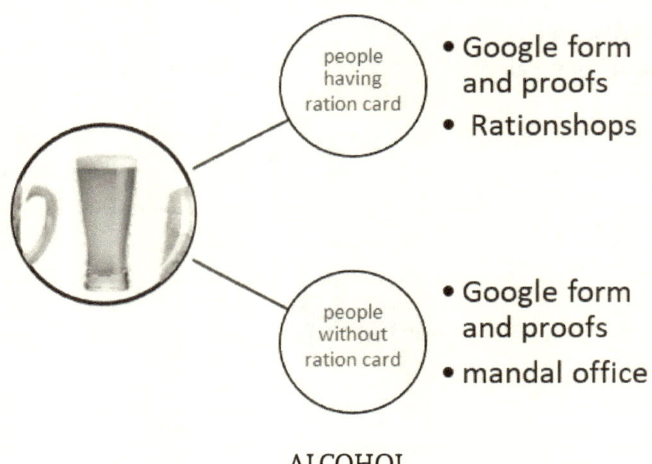

ALCOHOL

In this way, a person can reduce the amount of alcohol they take. This will reduce road accidents and domestic violence as well as provide people with a healthy level of alcohol.

Conclusion: -

"Alcohol is as addictive as raspberry, but it shows sadism in the body."

9.7 BEE CULTURE

Introduction and Analysis:

Many rely on beeswax and honey. The thing the government is going to do is support them.

- Safe kits will be provided to all those who depend on bees for their livelihood.
- Free education insurance and insurance for children will be arranged
- We also print book forms regarding apiculture in every school.

- We give free education and employment to their children under priority. This is because bees are the only ones that pollinate (pollinate) most of the trees, and most of us get what we need.
- We must protect such bees. If extinct, our whole earth would be empty, in vain, and life would be a mess. So, based on this, let's protect those who are working and living.
- We will provide them with safety and the necessary equipment they need. A doctor will be appointed in those places.

Conclusion: -

"These are the creatures that gave life to Jagannath."

9.8 HELPLINE Centres (Help Centres)

Word Introduction and Analysis: -

"People need to be made fully aware of everything their government has done. In most cases, help desks are being set up so that people can call the helpline and ask what their government is going to do, their problems, what they will do next year and full details of welfare schemes under the Right to Information Act. We set up help desks to provide information to the public regularly without any hassle."

HELP DESK

People can call the help desks and complain without any fear if there is any corruption, injustice or any problem. We are informing the authorities about the problem so that justice can be done to people.

Conclusion: -

"Do you know something about your life!!!! You can't look in the books for things that happen in your life, you are lazily about what the outside world is telling you."

9.9 BEGGAR FREE

Word Introduction: -

We see a lot of people begging, from small children to fruit crocodiles.

Content Analysis: -

According to 2011 statistics, the total number of beggars in India is male and female.

Beggars	male	female
413670	221673	191997

APPROX. BEGGARS IN INDIA

Percentage of beggars according to 2011 statistics = 413670 / 125,00,00,000 = 0.03%

The population we have taken is 10,00,00,000.

That is, the number of beggars in it = 0.03 / 100x 10,00,000 = 34000 (consider).

34000 beggars divided by age: -

S. No	age	% (consider)	number
1	0-14	20	6800.
2	15-65	70	23,800.
3	>65	10	3400.
	మొత్తం	100	34000.

BASED ON AGE

Our government seeks to take drastic action on this by dividing everyone by age and finding out who is begging for children up to the age of 14. If there is no parent or family member, then take them to an orphanage and give them new life. Those who are older than 65 will also have the mentality of working hard but age doesn't help them to do. if they do not have a family, they will be taken to old age home. We will take such people and teach them about the manufacturing process of indigenous goods and give them complete training on what they can do. We'll make them stand on their own two feet. All those between the ages of 15 and 65 will be counselled first and counselled a second time. If they still beg, we will give them a low-paying job in the municipal department. This means cleaning the road and removing dirty water.

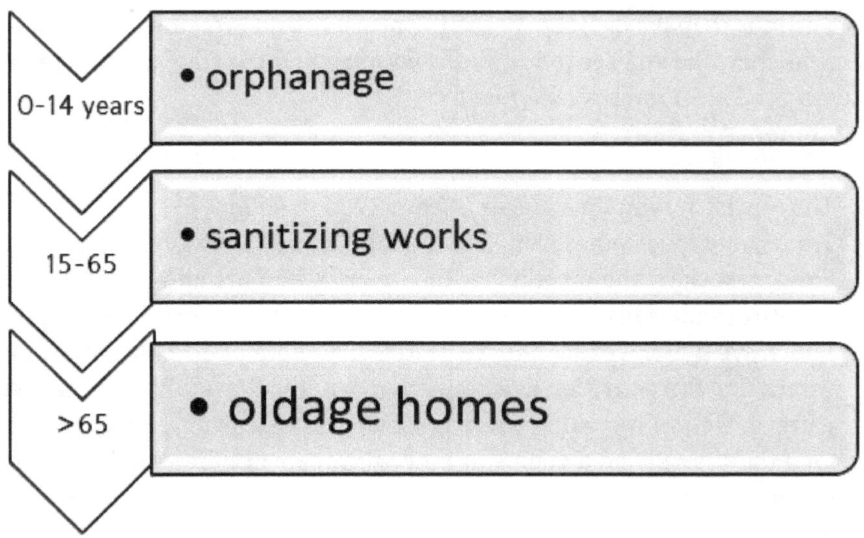

BEGGAR FREE

Through this, we will give them a job. That is why we have taken more. Until then, the temporary applies. We will only do a health check-up until it is permanent.

Conclusion: -

" The begging mind knows the problems that arise. We have to put an end to their problems."

9.10 TOURISM (Tourist Places)

Word Introduction: -

There are so many benefits to being in a tourist area. More money can also be raised. It can also attract a lot of foreigners. Although there are many good tourist destinations in our country, most governments do not spend money on them. The decision that is going to be taken by our government is that a lot of people will be fascinated by nature. Want to spend all day with nature. Starting a tourist area in the villages for them has given many people the opportunity to visit the villages with nature. Make sure to stay from morning to evening to attract families. That means being able to show every aspect of life that takes place in a village. Every four villages have to spend money for a nice decoration for a tourist spot in one place and see the law to gain the admiration of the people. This tourist area should be taken by private companies and the rooms should be well-developed with all new suggestions to make the most beautiful, pleasant and even night stays in the farm as they like and see to it that the country and the state and the region have a good economic development.

Content Analysis: -

- The tourist area in the villages is from 8 AM to 6 PM.
- Traditional food comes from a restaurant set up by the government.
- Foreigners start the morning with curd rice and are shown crop fields, beautiful waterfalls, and good places throughout the morning. Afternoon Lunch We will have lunch in the traditional manner and play afternoon games and fun activities. Even though it is in the Kartika Vana vasa meal pattern, we are repeating the ever-slowly disappearing pattern. All-day long they can spend a good fun time with their families. Book a slot for people in small doses and take good care of them. For this, the ticket price depends on the age.

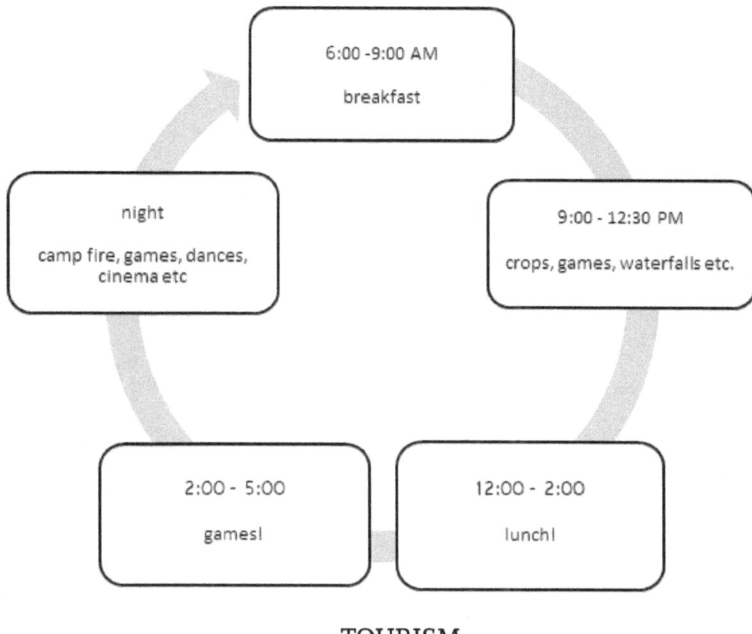

TOURISM

The main purpose is to better understand our tradition, our values and customs and to fill the state treasury for those who come to our state from different places.

Conclusion: -

"The truth is that nature is a beautiful chameleon, a beautiful group in one form or another in one place. Nature means Lakshmi, if you greet her, she will get addicted and give you whatever you want."

Thank you all,

Well, everyone appreciated it. The day had come. The assembly sessions would be in the next month.

I just asked my MLA and all cabinet ministers to undergo each law very carefully. I also told them as we were going on the right path, everyone would start to criticize us. So be careful.

The day before the Assembly sessions I was called by my assistant.

Hello!!!!!

Sir, this was the situation. What we had expected was not on its way. We were stopped by many external forces. They are all acting as a barrier for our laws. It's really bad news for us sir......

What?

I was baffled after hearing that news.............................

PART 2

www.ingramcontent.com/pod-product-compliance
Lightning Source LLC
Chambersburg PA
CBHW031406160726
47993CB00003B/1124